WALT WHITMAN

SONG OF MYSELF

PENGUIN BOOKS

PENGUIN BOOKS

Published by the Penguin Group
Penguin Books Ltd, 27 Wrights Lane, London W8 5TZ, England
Penguin Books USA Inc., 375 Hudson Street, New York, New York 10014, USA
Penguin Books Australia Ltd, Ringwood, Victoria, Australia
Penguin Books Canada Ltd, 10 Alcorn Avenue, Toronto, Ontario, Canada M4V 3B2
Penguin Books (NZ) Ltd, 182–190 Wairau Road, Auckland 10, New Zealand

Penguin Books Ltd, Registered Offices: Harmondsworth, Middlesex, England

This poem is from *The Complete Poems*, edited by
Francis Murphy, published in Penguin Classics 1986
This edition published 1995
1 3 5 7 9 10 8 6 4 2

Printed in England by Clays Ltd, St Ives plc

[1]
I celebrate myself,
And what I assume you shall assume,
For every atom belonging to me as good belongs to you.

I loafe and invite my soul,
I lean and loafe at my ease. . . . observing a spear of summer
	grass.

[2]
Houses and rooms are full of perfumes. . . . the shelves are
	crowded with perfumes,
I breathe the fragrance myself, and know it and like it,
The distillation would intoxicate me also, but I shall not let it.

The atmosphere is not a perfume. . . . it has no taste of the
	distillation. . . . it is odorless,
It is for my mouth forever. . . . I am in love with it,
I will go to the bank by the wood and become undisguised and
	naked,
I am mad for it to be in contact with me.

The smoke of my own breath,

Echoes, ripples, and buzzed whispers. . . . loveroot, silkthread, crotch and vine,

My respiration and inspiration. . . . the beating of my heart. . . . the passing of blood and air through my lungs,

The sniff of green leaves and dry leaves, and of the shore and darkcolored sea-rocks, and of hay in the barn,

The sound of the belched words of my voice. . . . words loosed to the eddies of the wind,

A few light kisses. . . . a few embraces. . . . a reaching around of arms,

The play of shine and shade on the trees as the supple boughs wag,

The delight alone or in the rush of the streets, or along the fields and hillsides,

The feeling of health. . . . the full-noon trill. . . . the song of me rising from bed and meeting the sun.

Have you reckoned a thousand acres much? Have you reckoned the earth much?

Have you practiced so long to learn to read?

Have you felt so proud to get at the meaning of poems?

Stop this day and night with me and you shall possess the origin of all poems,

You shall possess the good of the earth and sun. . . . there are millions of suns left,

You shall no longer take things at second or third hand. . . . nor look through the eyes of the dead. . . . nor feed on the spectres in books,

You shall not look through my eyes either, nor take things
    from me,
You shall listen to all sides and filter them from yourself.

[3]
I have heard what the talkers were talking.... the talk of the
    beginning and the end,
But I do not talk of the beginning or the end.

There was never any more inception than there is now,
Nor any more youth or age than there is now;
And will never be any more perfection than there is now,
Nor any more heaven or hell than there is now.

Urge and urge and urge,
Always the procreant urge of the world.

Out of the dimness opposite equals advance.... Always
    substance and increase,
Always a knit of identity.... always distinction.... always a
    breed of life.

To elaborate is no avail.... Learned and unlearned feel that it
    is so.

Sure as the most certain sure.... plumb in the uprights, well
    entretied, braced in the beams,
Stout as a horse, affectionate, haughty, electrical, I and this
    mystery here we stand.

Clear and sweet is my soul. . . . and clear and sweet is all that is not my soul.

Lack one lacks both. . . . and the unseen is proved by the seen,
Till that becomes unseen and receives proof in its turn.

Showing the best and dividing it from the worst, age vexes age,
Knowing the perfect fitness and equanimity of things, while they discuss I am silent, and go bathe and admire myself.

Welcome is every organ and attribute of me, and of any man hearty and clean,
Not an inch nor a particle of an inch is vile, and none shall be less familiar than the rest.

I am satisfied. . . . I see, dance, laugh, sing;
As God comes a loving bedfellow and sleeps at my side all night and close on the peep of the day,
And leaves for me baskets covered with white towels bulging the house with their plenty,
Shall I postpone my acceptation and realization and scream at my eyes,
That they turn from gazing after and down the road,
And forthwith cipher and show me to a cent,
Exactly the contents of one, and exactly the contents of two, and which is ahead?

4

[4]
Trippers and askers surround me,
People I meet.... the effect upon me of my early life.... of
    the war and city I live in.... of the nation,
The latest news.... discoveries, inventions, societies....
    authors old and new,
My dinner, dress, associates, looks, business, compliments,
    dues,
The real or fancied indifference of some man or woman I love,
The sickness of one of my folks—or of myself.... or ill-
    doing.... or loss or lack of money.... or depressions or
    exaltations,
They come to me days and nights and go from me again,
But they are not the Me myself.

Apart from the pulling and hauling stands what I am,
Stands amused, complacent, compassionating, idle, unitary,
Looks down, is erect, bends an arm on an impalpable certain
    rest,
Looks with its sidecurved head curious what will come next,
Both in and out of the game, and watching and wondering at
    it.

Backward I see in my own days where I sweated through fog
    with linguists and contenders,
I have no mockings or arguments.... I witness and wait.

5

I believe in you my soul.... the other I am must not abase
    itself to you,
And you must not be abased to the other.

Loafe with me on the grass.... loose the stop from your
    throat,
Not words, not music or rhyme I want.... not custom or
    lecture, not even the best,
Only the lull I like, the hum of your valved voice.

I mind how we lay in June, such a transparent summer
    morning;
You settled your head athwart my hips and gently turned over
    upon me,
And parted the shirt from my bosom-bone, and plunged your
    tongue to my barestript heart,
And reached till you felt my beard, and reached till you held
    my feet.

Swiftly arose and spread around me the peace and joy and
    knowledge that pass all the art and argument of the earth;
And I know that the hand of God is the elderhand of my own,
And I know that the spirit of God is the eldest brother of my
    own,
And that all the men ever born are also my brothers.... and
    the women my sisters and lovers,
And that a kelson of the creation is love;
And limitless are leaves stiff or drooping in the fields,

And brown ants in the little wells beneath them,
And mossy scabs of the wormfence, and heaped stones, and
    elder and mullen and pokeweed.

[6]
A child said, What is the grass? fetching it to me with full
    hands;
How could I answer the child?.... I do not know what it is
    any more than he.

I guess it must be the flag of my disposition, out of hopeful
    green stuff woven.

Or I guess it is the handkerchief of the Lord,
A scented gift and remembrancer designedly dropped,
Bearing the owner's name someway in the corners, that we
    may see and remark, and say Whose?

Or I guess the grass is itself a child.... the produced babe of
    the vegetation.

Or I guess it is a uniform hieroglyphic,
And it means, Sprouting alike in broad zones and narrow
    zones,
Growing among black folks as among white,
Kanuck, Tuckahoe, Congressman, Cuff, I give them the same,
    I receive them the same.

And now it seems to me the beautiful uncut hair of graves.

Tenderly will I use you curling grass,

It may be you transpire from the breasts of young men,
It may be if I had known them I would have loved them;
It may be you are from old people and from women, and from
    offspring taken soon out of their mothers' laps,
And here you are the mothers' laps.

This grass is very dark to be from the white heads of old
    mothers,
Darker than the colorless beards of old men,
Dark to come from under the faint red roofs of mouths.

O I perceive after all so many uttering tongues!
And I perceive they do not come from the roofs of mouths for
    nothing.

I wish I could translate the hints about the dead young men
    and women,
And the hints about old men and mothers, and the offspring
    taken soon out of their laps.

What do you think has become of the young and old men?
And what do you think has become of the women and
    children?

They are alive and well somewhere;
The smallest sprout shows there is really no death,
And if ever there was it led forward life, and does not wait at
    the end to arrest it,
And ceased the moment life appeared.

All goes onward and outward. . . . and nothing collapses,

And to die is different from what any one supposed, and
    luckier.

[7]
Has any one supposed it lucky to be born?
I hasten to inform him or her it is just as lucky to die, and I
    know it.
I pass death with the dying, and birth with the new-washed
    babe. . . . and am not contained between my hat and
    boots,
And peruse manifold objects, no two alike, and every one
    good,
The earth good, and the stars good, and their adjuncts all
    good.

I am not an earth nor an adjunct of an earth,
I am the mate and companion of people, all just as immortal
    and fathomless as myself;
They do not know how immortal, but I know.

Every kind for itself and its own. . . . for me mine male and
    female,
For me all that have been boys and that love women,
For me the man that is proud and feels how it stings to be
    slighted,
For me the sweetheart and the old maid. . . . for me mothers
    and the mothers of mothers,
For me lips that have smiled, eyes that have shed tears,
For me children and the begetters of children.

Who need be afraid of the merge?
Undrape. . . . you are not guilty to me, nor stale nor discarded,
I see through the broadcloth and gingham whether or no,
And am around, tenacious, acquisitive, tireless. . . . and can
    never be shaken away.

[8]
The little one sleeps in its cradle,
I lift the gauze and look a long time, and silently brush away
    flies with my hand.

The youngster and the redfaced girl turn aside up the bushy
    hill,
I peeringly view them from the top.

The suicide sprawls on the bloody floor of the bedroom,
It is so. . . . I witnessed the corpse. . . . there the pistol had
    fallen.

The blab of the pave. . . . the tires of carts and sluff of boot-
    soles and talk of the promenaders,
The heavy omnibus, the driver with his interrogating thumb,
    the clank of the shod horses on the granite floor,
The carnival of sleighs, the clinking and shouted jokes and
    pelts of snowballs;
The hurrahs for popular favorites. . . . the fury of roused
    mobs,
The flap of the curtained litter—the sick man inside, borne to
    the hospital,

The meeting of enemies, the sudden oath, the blows and fall,
The excited crowd—the policeman with his star quickly
working his passage to the centre of the crowd;
The impassive stones that receive and return so many echoes,
The souls moving along. . . . are they invisible while the least
atom of the stones is visible?
What groans of overfed or half-starved who fall on the flags
sunstruck or in fits,
What exclamations of women taken suddenly, who hurry
home and give birth to babes,
What living and buried speech is always vibrating here. . . .
what howls restrained by decorum,
Arrests of criminals, slights, adulterous offers made,
acceptances, rejections with convex lips,
I mind them or the resonance of them. . . . I come again and
again.

[9]
The big doors of the country-barn stand open and ready,
The dried grass of the harvest-time loads the slow-drawn
wagon,
The clear light plays on the brown gray and green intertinged,
The armfuls are packed to the sagging mow;
I am there. . . . I help. . . . I came stretched atop of the load,
I felt its soft jolts. . . . one leg reclined on the other,
I jump from the crossbeams, and seize the clover and timothy,
And roll head over heels, and tangle my hair full of wisps.

Alone far in the wilds and mountains I hunt,
Wandering amazed at my own lightness and glee,
In the late afternoon choosing a safe spot to pass the night,
Kindling a fire and broiling the freshkilled game,
Soundly falling asleep on the gathered leaves, my dog and gun
    by my side.

The Yankee clipper is under her three skysails. . . . she cuts the
    sparkle and scud,
My eyes settle the land. . . . I bend at her prow or shout
    joyously from the deck.

The boatmen and clamdiggers arose early and stopped for me,
I tucked my trowser-ends in my boots and went and had a
    good time,
You should have been with us that day round the chowder-
    kettle.

I saw the marriage of the trapper in the open air in the far-
    west. . . . the bride was a red girl,
Her father and his friends sat near by crosslegged and dumbly
    smoking. . . . they had moccasins to their feet and large
    thick blankets hanging from their shoulders;
On a bank lounged the trapper. . . . he was dressed mostly in
    skins. . . . his luxuriant beard and curls protected his neck,
One hand rested on his rifle. . . . the other hand held firmly the
    wrist of the red girl,
She had long eyelashes. . . . her head was bare. . . . her coarse

straight locks descended upon her voluptuous limbs and
reached to her feet.

The runaway slave came to my house and stopped outside,
I heard his motions crackling the twigs of the woodpile,
Through the swung half-door of the kitchen I saw him limpsey
    and weak,
And went where he sat on a log, and led him in and assured
    him,
And brought water and filled a tub for his sweated body and
    bruised feet,
And gave him a room that entered from my own, and gave
    him some coarse clean clothes.
And remember perfectly well his revolving eyes and his
    awkwardness,
And remember putting plasters on the galls of his neck and
    ankles;
He staid with me a week before he was recuperated and
    passed north,
I had him sit next me at table. . . . my firelock leaned in the
    corner.

[11]
Twenty-eight young men bathe by the shore,
Twenty-eight young men, and all so friendly,
Twenty-eight years of womanly life, and all so lonesome.

She owns the fine house by the rise of the bank,

She hides handsome and richly drest aft the blinds of the
      window.

Which of the young men does she like the best?
Ah the homeliest of them is beautiful to her.

Where are you off to, lady? for I see you,
You splash in the water there, yet stay stock still in your room.

Dancing and laughing along the beach came the twenty-ninth
      bather,
The rest did not see her, but she saw them and loved them.

The beards of the young men glistened with wet, it ran from
      their long hair,
Little streams passed all over their bodies.

An unseen hand also passed over their bodies,
It descended tremblingly from their temples and ribs.

The young men float on their backs, their white bellies swell to
      the sun. . . . they do not ask who seizes fast to them,
They do not know who puffs and declines with pendant and
      bending arch,
They do not think whom they souse with spray.

[12]
The butcher-boy puts off his killing-clothes, or sharpens his
      knife at the stall in the market,
I loiter enjoying his repartee and his shuffle and breakdown.
Blacksmiths with grimed and hairy chests environ the anvil,

14

Each has his main-sledge.... they are all out.... there is a
    great heat in the fire.

From the cinder-strewed threshold I follow their movements,
The lithe sheer of their waists plays even with their massive
    arms,
Overhand the hammers roll—overhand so slow—overhand so
    sure,
They do not hasten, each man hits in his place.

[13]
The negro holds firmly the reins of his four horses.... the
    block swags underneath on its tied-over chain,
The negro that drives the huge dray of the stoneyard....
    steady and tall he stands poised on one leg on the
    stringpiece,
His blue shirt exposes his ample neck and breast and loosens
    over his hipband,
His glance is calm and commanding.... he tosses the slouch
    of his hat away from his forehead,
The sun falls on his crispy hair and moustache.... falls on the
    black of his poilsh'd and perfect limbs.

I behold the picturesque giant and love him.... and I do not
    stop there,
I go with the team also.

In me the caresser of life wherever moving.... backward as
    well as forward slueing,

To niches aside and junior bending.

Oxen that rattle the yoke or halt in the shade, what is that you
    express in your eyes?
It seems to me more than all the print I have read in my life.

My tread scares the wood-drake and wood-duck on my distant
    and daylong ramble,
They rise together, they slowly circle around.
. . . . I believe in those winged purposes,
And acknowledge the red yellow and white playing within me,
And consider the green and violet and the tufted crown
    intentional;
And do not call the tortoise unworthy because she is not
    something else,
And the mocking bird in the swamp never studied the gamut,
    yet trills pretty well to me,
And the look of the bay mare shames silliness out of me.

[14]
The wild gander leads his flock through the cool night,
Ya-honk! he says, and sounds it down to me like an invitation;
The pert may suppose it meaningless, but I listen closer,
I find its purpose and place up there toward the November
    sky.

The sharphoofed moose of the north, the cat on the housesill,
    the chickadee, the prairie-dog,
The litter of the grunting sow as they tug at her teats,

The brood of the turkeyhen, and she with her halfspread
    wings,
I see in them and myself the same old law.

The press of my foot to the earth springs a hundred affections,
They scorn the best I can do to relate them.

I am enamoured of growing outdoors,
Of men that live among cattle or taste of the ocean or woods,
Of the builders and steerers of ships, of the wielders of axes
    and mauls, of the drivers of horses,
I can eat and sleep with them week in and week out.

What is commonest and cheapest and nearest and easiest is
    Me,
Me going in for my chances, spending for vast returns,
Adorning myself to bestow myself on the first that will take
    me,
Not asking the sky to come down to my goodwill,
Scattering it freely forever.

[15]
The pure contralto sings in the organloft,
The carpenter dresses his plank. . . . the tongue of his
    foreplane whistles its wild ascending lisp,
The married and unmarried children ride home to their
    thanksgiving dinner,
The pilot seizes the king-pin, he heaves down with a strong
    arm,

17

The mate stands braced in the whaleboat, lance and harpoon are ready,
The duck-shooter walks by silent and cautious stretches,
The deacons are ordained with crossed hands at the altar,
The spinning-girl retreats and advances to the hum of the big wheel,
The farmer stops by the bars of a Sunday and looks at the oats and rye,
The lunatic is carried at last to the asylum a confirmed case,
He will never sleep any more as he did in the cot in his mother's bedroom;
The jour printer with gray head and gaunt jaws works at his case,
He turns his quid of tobacco, his eyes get blurred with the manuscript;
The malformed limbs are tied to the anatomist's table,
What is removed drops horribly in a pail;
The quadroon girl is sold at the stand. . . . the drunkard nods by the barroom stove,
The machinist rolls up his sleeves. . . . the policeman travels his beat. . . . the gatekeeper marks who pass,
The young fellow drives the express-wagon. . . . I love him though I do not know him;
The half-breed straps on his light boots to compete in the race,
The western turkey-shooting draws old and young. . . . some lean on their rifles, some sit on logs,
Out from the crowd steps the marksman and takes his position and levels his piece;

The groups of newly-come immigrants cover the wharf or
    levee,
The wollypates hoe in the sugarfield, the coverseer views them
    from his saddle;
The bugle calls in the ballroom, the gentlemen run for their
    partners, the dancers bow to each other;
The youth lies awake in the cedar-roofed garret and harks to
    the musical rain,
The Wolverine sets traps on the creek that helps fill the Huron,
The reformer ascends the platform, he spouts with his mouth
    and nose,
The company returns from its excursion, the darkey brings up
    the rear and bears the well-riddled target,
The squaw wrapt in her yellow-hemmed cloth is offering
    moccasins and beadbags for sale,
The connoisseur peers along the exhibition-gallery with
    halfshut eyes bent sideways,
The deckhands make fast the steamboat, the plank is thrown
    for the shoregoing passengers,
The young sister holds out the skein, the elder sister winds it
    off in a ball and stops now and then for the knots,
The one-year wife is recovering and happy, a week ago she
    bore her first child,
The cleanhaired Yankee girl works with her sewing-machine or
    in the factory or mill,
The nine months' gone is in the parturition chamber, her
    faintness and pains are advancing;
The pavingman leans on his twohanded rammer—the

reporter's lead flies swiftly over the notebook—the
  signpainter is lettering with red and gold,
The canal-boy trots on the towpath—the bookkeeper counts at
  his desk—the shoemaker waxes his thread,
The conductor beats time for the band and all the performers
  follow him,
The child is baptised—the convert is making the first
  professions,
The regatta is spread on the bay. . . . how the white sails
  sparkle!
The drover watches his drove, he sings out to them that would
  stray,
The pedlar sweats with his pack on his back—the purchaser
  higgles about the odd cent,
The camera and plate are prepared, the lady must sit for her
  daguerreotype,
The bride unrumples her white dress, the minutehand of the
  clock moves slowly,
The opium eater reclines with rigid head and just-opened lips,
The prostitute draggles her shawl, her bonnet bobs on her
  tipsy and pimpled neck,
The crowd laugh at her blackguard oaths, the men jeer and
  wink to each other,
(Miserable! I do not laugh at your oaths nor jeer you,)
The President holds a cabinet council, he is surrounded by the
  great secretaries,
On the piazza walk five friendly matrons with twined arms;

The crew of the fish-smack pack repeated layers of halibut in
    the hold,
The Missourian crosses the plains toting his wares and his
    cattle,
The fare-collector goes through the train—he gives notice by
    the jingling of loose change,
The floormen are laying the floor—the tinners are tinning the
    roof—the masons are calling for mortar,
In single file each shouldering his hod pass onward the
    laborers;
Seasons pursuing each other the indescribable crowd is
    gathered. . . . it is the Fourth of July. . . . what salutes of
    cannon and small arms!
Seasons pursuing each other the plougher ploughs and the
    mower mows and the wintergrain falls in the ground;
Off on the lakes the pikefisher watches and waits by the hole
    in the frozen surface,
The stumps stand thick round the clearing, the squatter strikes
    deep with his axe,
The flatboatmen make fast toward dusk near the cottonwood
    or pekantrees,
The coon-seekers go now through the regions of the Red river,
    or through those drained by the Tennessee, or through
    those of the Arkansas,
The torches shine in the dark that hangs on the Chattahoochee
    or Altamahaw;
Patriachs sit at supper with sons and grandsons and great
    grandsons around them,

In walls of adobie, in canvas tents, rest hunters and trappers
after their day's sport.

The city sleeps and the country sleeps,
The living sleep for their time. . . . the dead sleep for their
time,
The old husband sleeps by his wife and the young husband
sleeps by his wife;
And these one and all tend inward to me, and I tend outward
to them,
And such as it is to be of these more or less I am.

[16]
I am of old and young, of the foolish as much as the
wise,
Regardless of others, ever regardful of others,
Maternal as well as paternal, a child as well as a man,
Stuffed with the stuff that is coarse, and stuffed with the stuff
that is fine,
One of the great nations, the nation of many nations—the
smallest the same and the largest the same,
A southerner soon as a northerner, a planter nonchalant and
hospitable,
A Yankee bound my own way. . . . ready for trade. . . . my
joints the limberest joints on earth and the sternest joints
on earth,
A Kentuckian walking the vale of the Elkhorn in my deerskin
leggings,

A boatman over the lakes or bays or along coasts. . . . a
    Hoosier, a Badger, a Buckeye,
A Louisianian or Georgian, a poke-easy from sandhills and
    pines,
At home on Canadian snowshoes or up in the bush, or with
    fishermen off Newfoundland,
At home in the fleet of iceboats, sailing with the rest and
    tacking,
At home on the hills of Vermont or in the woods of Maine or
    the Texan ranch,
Comrade of Californians. . . . comrade of free northwester-
    ners, loving their big proportions,
Comrade of raftsmen and coalmen—comrade of all who shake
    hands and welcome to drink and meat;
A learner with the simplest, a teacher of the thoughtfulest,
A novice beginning experient of myriads of seasons,
Of every hue and trade and rank, of every caste and religion,
Not merely of the New World but of Africa Europe or
    Asia. . . . a wandering savage,
A farmer, mechanic, or artist. . . . a gentleman, sailor, lover or
    quaker,
A prisoner, fancy-man, rowdy, lawyer, physician or priest.

I resist anything better than my own diversity,
And breathe the air and leave plenty after me,
And am not stuck up, and am in my place.

The moth and the fisheggs are in their place,
The suns I see and the suns I cannot see are in their place,

The palpable is in its place and the impalpable is in its place.

[17]
These are the thoughts of all men in all ages and lands, they
    are not original with me,
If they are not yours as much as mine they are nothing or next
    to nothing,
If they do not enclose everything they are next to nothing,
If they are not the riddle and the untying of the riddle they are
    nothing,
If they are not just as close as they are distant they are
    nothing.

This is the grass that grows wherever the land is and the water
    is,
This is the common air that bathes the globe.

This is the breath of laws and songs and behaviour,
This is the tasteless water of souls. . . . this is the true
    sustenance,
It is for the illiterate. . . . it is for the judges of the supreme
    court. . . . it is for the federal capitol and the state capitols,
It is for the admirable communes of literary men and
    composers and singers and lecturers and engineers and
    savans,
It is for the endless races of working people and farmers and
    seamen.

[18]

This is the trill of a thousand clear cornets and scream of the
    octave flute and strike of triangles.

I play not a march for victors only.... I play great marches
    for conquered and slain persons.

Have you heard that it was good to gain the day?
I also say it is good to fall.... battles are lost in the same
    spirit in which they are won.

I sound triumphal drums for the dead.... I fling through my
    embouchures the loudest and gayest music to them,
Vivas to those who have failed, and to those whose war-vessels
    sank in the sea, and those themselves who sank in the sea,
And to all generals that lost engagements, and all overcome
    heroes, and the numberless unknown heroes equal to the
    greatest heroes known.

[19]

This is the meal pleasantly set.... this is the meat and drink
    for natural hunger,
It is for the wicked just the same as the righteous.... I make
    appointments with all,
I will not have a single person slighted or left away,
The keptwoman and sponger and thief are hereby invited....
    the heavy-lipped slave is invited.... the venerealee is
    invited,
There shall be no difference between them and the rest.

This is the press of a bashful hand. . . . this is the float and
    odor of hair,
This is the touch of my lips to yours. . . . this is the murmur of
    yearning,
This is the far-off depth and height reflecting my own face,
This is the thoughtful merge of myself and the outlet again.

Do you guess I have some intricate purpose?
Well I have. . . . for the April rain has, and the mica on the
    side of a rock has.

Do you take it I would astonish?
Does the daylight astonish? or the early redstart twittering
    through the woods?
Do I astonish more than they?

This hour I tell things in confidence,
I might not tell everybody but I will tell you.

[20]
Who goes there! hankering, gross, mystical, nude?
How is it I extract strength from the beef I eat?

What is a man anyhow? What am I? and what are you?
All I mark as my own you shall offset it with your own,
Else it were time lost listening to me.

I do not snivel that snivel the world over,
That months are vacuums and the ground but wallow and
    filth,

That life is a suck and a sell, and nothing remains at the end
   but threadbare crape and tears.

Whimpering and truckling fold with powders for invalids. . . .
   conformity goes to the fourth-removed,
I cock my hat as I please indoors or out.

Shall I pray? Shall I venerate and be ceremonious?
I have pried through the strata and analyzed to a hair,
And counselled with doctors and calculated close and found
   no sweeter fat than sticks to my own bones.

In all people I see myself, none more and not one a barleycorn
   less,
And the good or bad I say or myself I say of them.

And I know I am solid and sound,
To me the converging objects of the universe perpetually flow,
All are written to me, and I must get what the writing means.

And I know I am deathless,
I know this orbit of mine cannot be swept by a carpenter's
   compass,
I know I shall not pass like a child's carlacue cut with a burnt
   stick at night.

I know I am august,
I do not trouble my spirit to vindicate itself or be understood,
I see that the elementary laws never apologize,
I reckon I behave no prouder than the level I plant my house
   by after all.

I exist as I am, that is enough,
If no other in the world be aware I sit content,
And if each and all be aware I sit content.

One world is aware, and by far the largest to me, and that is
myself,
And whether I come to my own today or in ten thousand or
ten million years,
I can cheerfully take it now, or with equal cheerfulness I can
wait.

My foothold is tenoned and mortised in granite,
I laugh at what you call dissolution,
And I know the amplitude of time.

[21]
I am the poet of the body,
And I am the poet of the soul.

The pleasures of heaven are with me, and the pains of hell are
with me,
The first I graft and increase upon myself. . . . the latter I
translate into a new tongue.

I am the poet of the woman the same as the man,
And I say it is as great to be a woman as to be a man,
And I say there is nothing greater than the mother of men.

I chant a new chant of dilation or pride,
We have had ducking and deprecating about enough,

I show that size is only development.

Have you outstript the rest? Are you the President?
It is a trifle. . . . they will more than arrive there every one, and
    still pass on.

I am he that walks with the tender and growing night;
I call to the earth and sea half-held by the night.

Press close barebosomed night! Press close magnetic
    nourishing night!
Night of south winds! Night of the large few stars!
Still nodding night! Mad naked summer night!

Smile O voluptuous coolbreathed earth!
Earth of the slumbering and liquid trees!
Earth of departed sunset! Earth of the mountains misty-topt!
Earth of the vitreous pour of the full moon just tinged with
    blue!
Earth of shine and dark mottling the tide of the river!
Earth of the limpid gray of clouds brighter and clearer for my
    sake!
Far-swooping elbowed earth! Rich apple-blossomed earth!
Smile, for your lover comes!

Prodigal! you have given me love!. . . . therefore I to you give
    love!
O unspeakable passionate love!

Thruster holding me tight and that I hold tight!

We hurt each other as the bridegroom and the bride hurt each
other.

[22]
You sea! I resign myself to you also.... I guess what you
mean,
I behold from the beach your crooked inviting fingers,
I believe you refuse to go back without feeling of me;
We must have a turn together.... I undress.... hurry me out
of sight of the land,
Cushion me soft.... rock me in billowy drowse,
Dash me with amorous wet.... I can repay you.

Sea of stretched ground-swells!
Sea breathing broad and convulsive breaths!
Sea of the brine of life! Sea of unshovelled and always-ready
graves!
Howler and scooper of storms! Capricious and dainty sea!
I am integral with you.... I too am of one phase and of all
phases.

Partaker of influx and efflux.... extoller of hate and
conciliation,
Extoller of amies and those that sleep in each other's arms.

I am he attesting sympathy;
Shall I make my list of things in the house and skip the house
that supports them?

I am the poet of commonsense and of the demonstrable and of
    immortality;
And am not the poet of goodness only. . . . I do not decline to
    be the poet of wickedness also.

Washes and razors for foofoos. . . . for me freckles and a
    bristling beard.

What blurt is it about virtue and about vice?
Evil propels me, and reform of evil propels me. . . . I stand
    indifferent,
My gait is no faultfinder's or rejecter's gait,
I moisten the roots of all that has grown.

Did you fear some scrofula out of the unflagging pregnancy?
Did you guess the celestial laws are yet to be worked over and
    rectified?

I step up to say that what we do is right and what we affirm
    is right. . . . and some is only the ore of right,
Witnesses of us. . . . one side a balance and the antipodal side
    a balance,
Soft doctrine as steady help as stable doctrine,
Thoughts and deeds of the present our rouse and early start.

This minute that comes to me over the past decillions,
There is no better than it and now.

What behaved well in the past or behaves well today is not
    such a wonder,

The wonder is always and always how there can be a mean
 man or an infidel.

[23]
Endless unfolding of words of ages!
And mine a word of the modern. . . . a word en masse.

A word of the faith that never balks,
One time as good as another time. . . . here or henceforward it
 is all the same to me.

A word of reality. . . . materialism first and last imbuing.

Hurrah for positive science! Long live exact demonstration!
Fetch stonecrop and mix it with cedar and branches of lilac;
This is the lexicographer or chemist. . . . this made a grammar
 of the old cartouches,
These mariners put the ship through dangerous unknown seas,
This is the geologist, and this works with the scalpel, and this
 is a mathematician.

Gentlemen I receive you, and attach and clasp hands with you,
The facts are useful and real. . . . they are not my dwelling. . . .
 I enter by them to an area of the dwelling.

I am less the reminder of property or qualities, and more the
 reminder of life,
And go on the square for my own sake and for other's sake,
And make short account of neuters and geldings, and favor
 men and women fully equipped,

And beat the gong of revolt, and stop with fugitives and them
that plot and conspire.

[24]
Walt Whitman, an American, one of the roughs, a kosmos,
Disorderly fleshy and sensual. . . . eating drinking and
breeding,
No sentimentalist. . . . no stander above men and women or
apart from them. . . . no more modest than immodest.

Unscrew the locks from the doors!
Unscrew the doors themselves from their jambs!

Whoever degrades another degrades me. . . . and whatever is
done or said returns at last to me,
And whatever I do or say I also return.

Through me the afflatus surging and surging. . . . through me
the current and index.

I speak the password primeval. . . . I give the sign of
democracy;
By God! I will accept nothing which all cannot have their
counterpart of on the same terms.

Through me many long dumb voices,
Voices of the interminable generations of slaves,
Voices of prostitutes and of deformed persons,
Voices of the diseased and despairing, and of thieves and
dwarfs,

Voices of cycles of preparation and accretion,
And of the threads that connect the stars—and of wombs, and
    of the fatherstuff,
And of the rights of them the others are down upon,
Of the trivial and flat and foolish and despised,
Of fog in the air and beetles rolling balls of dung.

Through me forbidden voices,
Voices of sexes and lusts. . . . voices veiled, and I remove the
    veil,
Voices indecent by me clarified and transfigured.

I do not press my finger across my mouth,
I keep as delicate around the bowels as around the head and
    heart,
Copulation is no more rank to me than death is.

I believe in the flesh and the appetites,
Seeing hearing and feeling are miracles, and each part and tag
    of me is a miracle.

Divine am I inside and out, and I make holy whatever I touch
    or am touched from;
The scent of these arm-pits is aroma finer than prayer,
This head is more than churches or bibles or creeds.

If I worship any particular thing it shall be some of the spread
    of my body;
Translucent mould of me it shall be you,
Shaded ledges and rests, firm masculine coulter, it shall be you,

Whatever goes to the tilth of me it shall be you,
You my rich blood, your milky stream pale strippings of my
    life;
Breast that presses against other breasts it shall be
    you,
My brain it shall be your occult convolutions,
Root of washed sweet-flag, timorous pond-snipe, nest of
    guarded duplicate eggs, it shall be you,
Mixed tussled hay of head and beard and brawn it shall be
    you;
Trickling sap of maple, fibre of manly wheat, it shall be you;
Sun so generous it shall be you,
Vapors lighting and shading my face it shall be you,
You sweaty brooks and dews it shall be you,
Winds whose soft-tickling genitals rub against me it shall be
    you,
Broad muscular fields, branches of liveoak, loving lounger in
    my winding paths, it shall be you,
Hands I have taken, face I have kissed, mortal I have ever
    touched, it shall be you.

I dote on myself. . . . there is that lot of me, and all so luscious,
Each moment and whatever happens thrills me with joy.

I cannot tell how my ankles bend. . . . nor whence the cause of
    my faintest wish,
Nor the cause of the friendship I emit. . . . nor the cause of the
    friendship I take again.

To walk up my stoop is unaccountable. . . . I pause to consider
    if it really be,
That I eat and drink is spectacle enough for the great authors
    and schools,
A morning-glory at my window satisfies me more than the
    metaphysics of books.

To behold the daybreak!
The little light fades the immense and diaphanous shadows,
The air tastes good to my palate.

Hefts of the moving world at innocent gambols, silently rising,
    freshly exuding,
Scooting obliquely high and low.

Something I cannot see puts upward libidinous prongs,
Seas of bright juice suffuse heaven.

The earth by the sky staid with. . . . the daily close of their
    junction,
The heaved challenge from the east that moment over my
    head,
The mocking taunt, See then whether you shall be master!

[25]
Dazzling and tremendous how quick the sunrise would kill me,
If I could not now and always send sunrise out of me.

We also ascend dazzling and tremendous as the sun,

We found our own my soul in the calm and cool of the
    daybreak.

My voice goes after what my eyes cannot reach,
With the twirl of my tongue I encompass worlds and volumes
    of worlds.

Speech is the twin of my vision. . . . it is unequal to measure
    itself.

It provokes me forever,
It says sarcastically, Walt, you understand enough. . . . why
    don't you let it out then?

Come now I will not be tantalized. . . . you conceive too much
    of articulation.

Do you not know how the buds beneath are folded?
Waiting in gloom protected by frost,
The dirt receding before my prophetical screams,
I underlying causes to balance them at last,
My knowledge my live parts. . . . it keeping tally with the
    meaning of things,
Happiness. . . . which whoever hears me let him or her set out
    in search of this day.

My final merit I refuse you. . . . I refuse putting from me the
    best I am.

Encompass worlds but never try to encompass me,
I crowd your noisiest talk by looking toward you.

Writing and talk do not prove me,
I carry the plenum of proof and every thing else in my face,
With the hush of my lips I confound the topmost skeptic.

[26]
I think I will do nothing for a long time but listen,
And accrue what I hear into myself. . . . and let sounds
    contribute toward me.

I hear the bravuras of birds. . . . the bustle of growing wheat. . . .
    gossip of flames. . . . clack of sticks cooking my meals.

I hear the sound of the human voice. . . . a sound I love,
I hear all sounds as they are tuned to their uses. . . . sounds of
    the city and sounds out of the city. . . . sounds of the day
    and night;
Talkative young ones to those that like them. . . . the recitative
    of fish-pedlars and fruit-pedlars. . . . the loud laugh of
    workpeople at their meals,
The angry base of disjointed friendship. . . . the faint tones of
    the sick,
The judge with hands tight to the desk, his shaky lips
    pronouncing a death-sentence,
The heave'e'yo of stevedores unlading ships by the wharves. . . .
    the refrain of the anchor-lifters;
The ring of alarm-bells. . . . the cry of fire. . . . the whirr of
    swift-streaking engines and hose-carts with premonitory
    tinkles and colored lights,

The steam-whistle. . . . the solid roll of the train of
    approaching cars;
The slow-march played at night at the head of the association,
They go to guard some corpse. . . . the flag-tops are draped
    with black muslin.

I hear the violincello or man's heart complaint,
And hear the keyed cornet or else the echo of sunset.

I hear the chorus. . . . it is a grand-opera. . . . this indeed is
    music!

A tenor large and fresh as the creation fills me,
The orbic flex of his mouth is pouring and filling me full.

I hear the trained soprano. . . . she convulses me like the
    climax of my love-grip;
The orchestra whirls me wider than Uranus flies,
It wrenches unnamable ardors from my breast,
It throbs me to gulps of the farthest down horror,
It sails me. . . . I dab with bare feet. . . . they are licked by the
    indolent waves,
I am exposed. . . . cut by bitter and poisoned hail,
Steeped amid honeyed morphine.. . . . my windpipe squeezed
    in the fakes of death,
Let up again to feel the puzzle of puzzles,
And that we call Being.

[27]
To be in any form, what is that?
If nothing lay more developed the quahaug and its callous shell
    were enough.

Mine is no callous shell,
I have instant conductors all over me whether I pass or stop,
They seize every object and lead it harmlessly through me.

I merely stir, press, feel with my fingers, and am happy,
To touch my person to some one else's is about as much as I
    can stand.

[28]
Is this then a touch? . . . . quivering me to a new identity,
Flames and ether making a rush for my veins,
Treacherous tip of me reaching and crowding to help them,
My flesh and blood playing out lightning, to strike what is
    hardly different from myself,
On all sides prurient provokers stiffening my limbs,
Straining the udder of my heart for its withheld drip,
Behaving licentious toward me, taking no denial,
Depriving me of my best as for a purpose,
Unbuttoning my clothes and holding me by the bare waist,
Deluding my confusion with the calm of the sunlight and
    pasture fields,
Immodestly sliding the fellow-senses away,
They bribed to swap off with touch, and go and graze at the
    edges of me,

No consideration, no regard for my draining strength or my
    anger,
Fetching the rest of the herd around to enjoy them awhile,
Then all uniting to stand on a headland and worry me.

The sentries desert every other part of me,
They have left me helpless to a red marauder,
They all come to the headland to witness and assist against
    me.

I am given up by traitors;
I talk wildly. . . . I have lost my wits. . . . I and nobody else am
    the greatest traitor,
I went myself first to the headland. . . . my own hands carried
    me there.

You villain touch! what are you doing?. . . . my breath is tight
    in its throat;
Unclench your floodgates! you are too much for me.

[29]
Blind loving wrestling touch! Sheathed hooded sharptoothed
    touch!
Did it make you ache so leaving me?

Parting tracked by arriving. . . . perpetual payment of the
    perpetual loan,
Rich showering rain, and recompense richer afterward.

Sprouts take and accumulate. . . . stand by the curb prolific
  and vital,
Landscapes projected masculine full-sized and golden.

[30]
All truths wait in all things,
They neither hasten their own delivery nor resist it,
They do not need the obstetric forceps of the surgeon,
The insignificant is as big to me as any,
What is less or more than a touch?

Logic and sermons never convince,
The damp of the night drives deeper into my soul.

Only what proves itself to every man and woman is so,
Only what nobody denies is so.

A minute and a drop of me settle my brair;
I believe the soggy clods shall become lovers and lamps,
And a compend of compends is the meat of a man or woman,
And a summit and flower there is the feeling they have for
  each other,
And they are to branch boundlessly out of that lesson until it
  becomes omnific,
And until every one shall delight us, and we them.

[31]
I believe a leaf of grass is no less than the journeywork of the
  stars,

And the pismire is equally perfect, and a grain of sand, and the
    egg of the wren,
And the tree-toad is a chef-d'oeuvre for the highest,
And the running blackberry would adorn the parlors of
    heaven,
And the narrowest hinge in my hand puts to scorn all
    machinery,
And the cow crunching with depressed head surpasses any
    statue,
And a mouse is miracle enough to stagger sextillions of
    infidels,
And I could come every afternoon of my life to look at the
    farmer's girl boiling her iron tea-kettle and baking
    shortcake.

I find I incorporate gneiss and coal and long-threaded moss
    and fruits and grains and esculent roots,
And am stucco'd with quadrupeds and birds all over,
And have distanced what is behind me for good reasons,
And call any thing close again when I desire it.

In vain the speeding or shyness,
In vain the plutonic rocks send their old heat against my
    approach,
In vain the mastodon retreats beneath its own powdered
    bones,
In vain objects stand leagues off and assume manifold shapes,
In vain the ocean settling in hollows and the great monsters
    lying low,

In vain the buzzard houses herself with the sky,
In vain the snake slides through the creepers and logs,
In vain the elk takes to the inner passes of the woods,
In vain the razorbilled auk sails far north to Labrador,
I follow quickly. . . . I ascend to the nest in the fissure of the
    cliff.

[32]
I think I could turn and live awhile with the animals. . . . they
    are so placid and self-contained,
I stand and look at them sometimes half the day long.

They do not sweat and whine about their condition,
They do not lie awake in the dark and weep for their sins,
They do not make me sick discussing their duty to God,
Not one is dissatisfied. . . . not one is demented with the mania
    of owning things,
Not one kneels to another nor to his kind that lived thousands
    of years ago,
Not one is respectable or industrious over the whole earth.

So they show their relations to me and I accept them;
They bring me tokens of myself. . . . they evince them plainly
    in their possession.

I do not know where they got those tokens,
I must have passed that way untold times ago and negligently
    dropt them,
Myself moving forward then and now and forever,

Gathering and showing more always and with velocity,
Infinite and omnigenous and the like of these among them;
Not too exclusive toward the reachers of my remembrancers,
Picking out here one that shall be my amie,
Choosing to go with him on brotherly terms.

A gigantic beauty of a stallion, fresh and responsive to my
    caresses,
Head high in the forehead and wide between the ears,
Limbs glossy and supple, tail dusting the ground,
Eyes well apart and full of sparkling wickedness. . . . ears
    finely cut and flexibly moving.

His nostrils dilate. . . . my heels embrace him. . . . his well built
    limbs tremble with pleasure. . . . we speed around and
    return.

I but use you a moment and then I resign you stallion. . . . and
    do not need your paces, and outgallop them,
And myself as I stand or sit pass faster than you.

[33]
Swift wind! Space! My Soul! Now I know it is true what I
    guessed at;
What I guessed when I loafed on the grass,
What I guessed while I lay alone in my bed. . . . and again as
    I walked the beach under the paling stars of the morning.

My ties and ballasts leave me. . . . I travel. . . . I sail. . . . my
    elbows rest in the sea-gaps,

I skirt the sierras. . . . my palms cover continents,
I am afoot with my vision.

By the city's quadrangular houses. . . . in log-huts, or camping
    with lumbermen,
Along the ruts of the turnpike. . . . along the dry gulch and
    rivulet bed,
Hoeing my onion-patch, and rows of carrots and parsnips. . . .
    crossing savannas. . . . trailing in forests,
Prospecting. . . . gold-digging. . . . girdling the trees of a new
    purchase,
Scorched ankle-deep by the hot sand. . . . hauling my boat
    down the shallow river;
Where the panther walks to and fro on a limb overhead. . . .
    where the buck turns furiously at the hunter,
Where the rattlesnake suns his flabby length on a rock. . . .
    where the otter is feeding on fish,
Where the alligator in his tough pimples sleeps by the bayou,
Where the black bear is searching for roots or honey. . . .
    where the beaver pats the mud with his paddle-tail;
Over the growing sugar. . . . over the cottonplant. . . . over the
    rice in its low moist field;
Over the sharp-peaked farmhouse with its scalloped scum and
    slender shoots from the gutters;
Over the western persimmon. . . . over the longleaved corn and
    the delicate blue-flowered flax;
Over the white and brown buckwheat, a hummer and a buzzer
    there with the rest,

46

Over the dusky green of the rye as it ripples and shades in the
    breeze;
Scaling mountains.... pulling myself cautiously up.....
    holding on by low scragged limbs,
Walking the path worn in the grass and beat through the
    leaves of the brush;
Where the quail is whistling betwixt the woods and the
    wheatlot,
Where the bat flies in the July eve.... where the great goldbug
    drops through the dark;
Where the flails keep time on the barn floor,
Where the brook puts out of the roots of the old tree and
    flows to the meadow,
Where cattle stand and shake away flies with the tremulous
    shuddering of their hides,
Where the cheese-cloth hangs in the kitchen, and andirons
    straddle the hearth-slab, and cobwebs fall in festoons
    from the rafters;
Where triphammers crash.... where the press is whirling its
    cylinders;
Wherever the human heart beats with terrible throes out of its
    ribs;
Where the pear-shaped balloon is floating aloft.... floating in
    it myself and looking composedly down;
Where the life-car is drawn on the slipnoose.... where the
    heat hatches pale-green eggs in the dented sand,
Where the she-whale swims with her calves and never forsakes
    them,

Where the steamship trails hindways its long pennant of smoke,

Where the ground-shark's fin cuts like a black chip out of the water,

Where the half-burned brig is riding on unknown currents,

Where shells grow to her slimy deck, and the dead are corrupting below;

Where the striped and starred flag is borne at the head of the regiments;

Approaching Manhattan, up by the long-stretching island,

Under Niagara, the cataract falling like a veil over my countenance;

Upon a door-step. . . . upon the horse-block of hard wood outside,

Upon the race-course, or enjoying pic-nics or jigs or a good game of base-ball,

At he-festivals with blackguard jibes and ironical license and bull-dances and drinking and laughter,

At the cider-mill, tasting the sweet of the brown sqush. . . . sucking the juice through a straw,

At apple-peelings, wanting kisses for all the red fruit I find,

At musters and beach-parties and friendly bees and huskings and house-raisings;

Where the mockingbird sounds his delicious gurgles, and cackles and screams and weeps,

Where the hay-rick stands in the barnyard, and the dry-stalks are scattered, and the brood cow waits in the hovel,

Where the bull advances to do his masculine work, and the
stud to the mare, and the cock is treading the hen,
Where the heifers browse, and the geese nip their food with
short jerks;
Where the sundown shadows lengthen over the limitless and
lonesome prairie,
Where the herds of buffalo make a crawling spread of the
square miles far and near;
Where the hummingbird shimmers. . . . where the neck of
the longlived swan is curving and winding;
Where the laughing-gull scoots by the slappy shore and laughs
her near-human laugh;
Where beehives range on a gray bench in the garden half-hid
by the high weeds;
Where the band-necked partridges roost in a ring on the
ground with their heads out;
Where burial coaches enter the arched gates of a cemetery;
Where winter wolves bark amid wastes of snow and icicled
trees;
Where the yellow-crowned heron comes to the edge of the
marsh at night and feeds upon small crabs;
Where the splash of swimmers and divers cools the warm
noon;
Where the katydid works her chromatic reed on the walnut-
tree over the well;
Through patches of citrons and cucumbers with silver-wired
leaves,

Through the salt-lick or orange glade.... or under conical
   firs;
Through the gymnasium..... through the curtained
   saloon.... through the office or public hall;
Pleased with the native and pleased with the foreign....
   pleased with the new and old,
Pleased with women, the homely as well as the handsome,
Pleased with the quakeress as she puts off her bonnet and talks
   melodiously,
Pleased with the primitive tunes of the choir of the
   whitewashed church,
Pleased with the earnest words of the sweating Methodist
   preacher, or any preacher.... looking seriously at the
   camp-meeting;
Looking in at the shop-windows in Broadway the whole
   forenoon.... pressing the flesh of my nose to the thick
   plate-glass,
Wandering the same afternoon with my face turned up to the
   clouds;
My right and left arms round the sides of two friends and I in
   the middle;
Coming home with the bearded and dark-cheeked bush-
   boy.... riding behind him at the drape of the day;
Far from the settlements studying the print of animals' feet, or
   the moccasin print;
By the cot in the hospital reaching lemonade to a feverish
   patient,

By the coffined corpse when all is still, examining with a
     candle;
Voyaging to every port to dicker and adventure;
Hurrying with the modern crowd, as eager and fickle as any,
Hot toward one I hate, ready in my madness to knife him;
Solitary at midnight in my back yard, my thoughts gone from
     me a long while,
Walking the old hills of Judea with the beautiful gentle god by
     my side;
Speeding through space. . . . speeding through heaven and
     the stars,
Speeding amid the seven satellites and the broad ring and the
     diameter of eighty thousand miles,
Speeding with tailed meteors. . . . throwing fire-balls like the
     rest,
Carrying the crescent child that carries its own full mother in
     its belly:
Storming enjoying planning loving cautioning,
Backing and filling, appearing and disappearing,
I tread day and night such roads.

I visit the orchards of God and look at the spheric product,
And look at quintillions ripened, and look at quintillions
     green.

I fly the flight of the fluid and swallowing soul,
My course runs below the soundings of plummets.

I help myself to material and immaterial,

No guard can shut me off, no law can prevent me.

I anchor my ship for a little while only,
My messengers continually cruise away or bring their returns
    to me.

I go hunting polar furs and the seal. . . . leaping chasms with
    a pike-pointed staff. . . . clinging to topples of brittle and
    blue.

I ascend to the foretruck. . . . I take my place late at night in
    the crow's nest. . . . we sail through the arctic sea. . . . it is
    plenty light enough,
Through the clear atmosphere I stretch around on the
    wonderful beauty,
The enormous masses of ice pass me and I pass them. . . . the
    scenery is plain in all directions,
The white-topped mountains point up in the distance. . . . I
    fling out my fancies toward them;
We are about approaching some great battlefield in which we
    are soon to be engaged,
We pass the colossal outposts of the encampment. . . . we pass
    with still feet and caution;
Or we are entering by the suburbs some vast and ruined
    city. . . . the blocks and fallen architecture more than all
    the living cities of the globe.

I am a free companion. . . . I bivouac by invading watchfires.

I turn the bridegroom out of bed and stay with the bride
    myself,
And tighten her all night to my thighs and lips.

My voice is the wife's voice, the screech by the rail of the
    stairs,
They fetch my man's body up dripping and drowned.

I understand the large hearts of heroes,
The courage of present times and all times;
How the skipper saw the crowded and rudderless wreck of the
    steamship, and death chasing it up and down the storm,
How he knuckled tight and gave not back one inch, and was
    faithful of days and faithful of nights,
And chalked in large letters on a board, Be of good cheer, We
    will not desert you;
How he saved the drifting company at last,
How the lank loose-gowned women looked when boated from
    the side of their prepared graves,
How the silent old-faced infants, and the lifted sick, and the
    sharp-lipped unshaved men;
All this I swallow and it tastes good. . . . I like it well, and it
    becomes mine,
I am the man. . . . I suffered. . . . I was there.

The disdain and calmness of martyrs,
The mother condemned for a witch and burnt with dry wood,
    and her children gazing on;

The hounded slave that flags in the race and leans by the
    fence, blowing and covered with sweat,
The twinges that sting like needles his legs and neck,
The murderous buckshot and the bullets,
All these I feel or am.

I am the hounded slave.... I wince at the bite of the dogs,
Hell and despair are upon me.... crack and again crack the
    marksmen,
I clutch the rails of the fence.... my gore dribs thinned with
    the ooze of my skin,
I fall on the weeds and stones,
The riders spur their unwilling horses and haul close,
They taunt my dizzy ears.... they beat me violently over the
    head with their whip-stocks.

Agonies are one of my changes of garments;
I do not ask the wounded person how he feels.... I myself
    become the wounded person,
My hurt turns livid upon me as I lean on a cane and observe.

I am the mashed fireman with breastbone broken... tumbling
    walls buried me in their debris,
Heat and smoke I inspired.... I heard the yelling shouts of
    my comrades,
I heard the distant click of their picks and shovels;
They have cleared the beams away.... they tenderly lift me
    forth.

I lie in the night air in my red shirt. . . . the pervading hush is
    for my sake,
Painless after all I lie, exhausted but not so unhappy,
White and beautiful are the faces around me. . . . the heads are
    bared of their fire-caps,
The kneeling crowd fades with the light of the torches.

Distant and dead resuscitate,
They show as the dial or move as the hands of me. . . . and I
    am the clock myself.

I am an old artillerist, and tell of some fort's
    bombardment. . . . and am there again.

Again the reveille of drummers. . . . again the attacking cannon
    and mortars and howitzers,
Again the attacked send their cannon responsive.

I take part. . . . I see and hear the whole,
The cries and curses and roar. . . . the plaudits for well aimed
    shots,
The ambulanza slowly passing the trailing its red drip,
Workmen searching after damages and to make indispensable
    repairs,
The fall of grenades through the rent roof. . . . the fan-shaped
    explosion,
The whizz of limbs heads stone wood and iron high in the air.

Again gurgles the mouth of my dying general. . . . he furiously
    waves with his hand,

He gasps through the clot. . . . Mind not me. . . . mind. . . . the
    entrenchments.

[34]
I tell not the fall of Alamo. . . . not one escaped to tell the fall
    of Alamo,
The hundred and fifty are dumb yet at Alamo.

Hear now the tale of a jetblack sunrise,
Hear of the murder in cold blood of four hundred and twelve
    young men.

Retreating they had formed in a hollow square with their
    baggage for breastworks,
Nine hundred lives out of the surrounding enemy's nine times
    their number was the price they took in advance,
Their colonel was wounded and their ammunition gone,
They treated for an honorable capitulation, received writing
    and seal, gave up their arms, and marched back prisoners
    of war.

They were the glory of the race of rangers,
Matchless with a horse, a rifle, a song, a supper or a courtship,
Large, turbulent, brave, handsome, generous, proud and
    affectionate,
Bearded, sunburnt, dressed in the free costume of hunters,
Not a single one over thirty years of age.

The second Sunday morning they were brought out in squads
    and massacred. . . . it was beautiful early summer,

The work commenced about five o'clock and was over by
    eight.

None obeyed the command to kneel,
Some made a mad and helpless rush. . . . some stood stark and
    straight,
A few fell at once, shot in the temple or heart. . . . the living
    and dead lay together,
The maimed and mangled dug in the dirt. . . . the new-comers
    saw them there;
Some half-killed attempted to crawl away,
These were dispatched with bayonets or battered with the
    blunts of muskets;
A youth not seventeen years old seized his assassin till two
    more came to release him,
The three were all torn, and covered with the boy's blood.

At eleven o'clock began the burning of the bodies;
And that is the tale of the murder of the four hundred and
    twelve young men,
And that was a jetblack sunrise.

[35]
Did you read in the seabooks of the oldfashioned frigate-fight?
Did you learn who won by the light of the moon and stars?

Our foe was no skulk in his ship, I tell you,
His was the English pluck, and there is no tougher or truer,
    and never was, and never will be;

Along the lowered eve he came, horribly raking us.

We closed with him. . . . the yards entangled. . . . the cannon touched,
My captain lashed fast with his own hands.

We had received some eighteen-pound shots under the water,
On our lower-gun-deck two large pieces had burst at the first fire, killing all around and blowing up overhead.

Ten o'clock at night, and the full moon shining and the leaks on the gain, and five feet of water reported,
The master-at-arms loosing the prisoners confined in the after-hold to give them a chance for themselves.

The transit to and from the magazine was now stopped by the sentinels,
They saw so many strange faces they did not know whom to trust.

Our frigate was afire. . . . the other asked if we demanded quarters? if our colors were struck and the fighting done?

I laughed content when I heard the voice of my little captain,
We have not struck, he composedly cried, We have just begun our part of the fighting.

Only three guns were in use,
One was directed by the captain himself against the enemy's mainmast,

Two well-served with grape and canister silenced his musketry
and cleared his decks.

The tops alone seconded the fire of this little battery, especially
the maintop,
They all held out bravely during the whole of the action.

Not a moment's cease,
The leaks gained fast on the pumps. . . . the fire eat toward the
powder-magazine,
One of the pumps was shot away. . . . it was generally thought
we were sinking.

Serene stood the little captain,
He was not hurried. . . . his voice was neither high nor low,
His eyes gave more light to us than our battle-lanterns.

Toward twelve at night, there in the beams of the moon they
surrendered to us.

[36]
Stretched and still lay the midnight,
Two great hulls motionless on the breast of the darkness,
Our vessel riddled and slowly sinking. . . . preparations to pass
to the one we had conquered,
The captain on the quarter deck coldly giving his orders
through a countenance white as a sheet,
Near by the corpse of the child that served in the cabin,
The dead face of an old salt with long white hair and carefully
curled whiskers,

The flames spite of all that could be done flickering aloft and
    below,
The husky voices of the two or three officers yet fit for duty,
Formless stacks of bodies and bodies by themselves. . . . dabs
    of flesh upon the masts and spars,
The cut of cordage and dangle of rigging. . . . the slight shock
    of the soothe of waves,
Black and impassive guns, and litter of powder-parcels, and
    the strong scent,
Delicate sniffs of the seabreeze. . . . smells of sedgy grass and
    fields by the shore. . . . death-messages given in charge to
    survivors,
The hiss of the surgeon's knife and the gnawing teeth of his
    saw,
The wheeze, the cluck, the swash of falling blood. . . . the
    short wild scream, the long dull tapering groan,
These so. . . . these irretrievable.

[37]
O Christ! My fit is mastering me!
What the rebel said gaily adjusting his throat to the rope-
    noose,
What the savage at the stump, his eye-sockets empty, his
    mouth spirting whoops and defiance,
What stills the traveler come to the vault at Mount Vernon,
What sobers the Brooklyn boy as he looks down the shores of
    the Wallabout and remembers the prison ships,

What burnt the gums of the redcoat at Saratoga when he
    surrendered his brigades,
These become mine and me every one, and they are but little,
I become as much more as I like.

I become any presence or truth of humanity here,
And see myself in prison shaped like another man,
And feel the dull unintermitted pain.

For me the keepers of convicts shoulder their carbines and
    keep watch,
It is I let out in the morning and barred at night.

Not a mutineer walks handcuffed to the jail, but I am
    handcuffed to him and walk by his side,
I am less the jolly one there, and more the silent one with
    sweat on my twitching lips.

Not a youngster is taken for larceny, but I go too and am tried
    and sentenced.

Not a cholera patient lies at the last gasp, but I also lie at the
    last gasp,
My face is ash-colored, my sinews gnarl. . . . away from me
    people retreat.

Askers embody themselves in me, and I am embodied in them,
I project my hat and sit shamefaced and beg.

I rise extatic through all, and sweep with the true gravitation,
The whirling and whirling is elemental within me.

[38]
Somehow I have been stunned. Stand back!
Give me a little time beyond my cuffed head and slumbers and
  dreams and gaping,
I discover myself on a verge of the usual mistake.

That I could forget the mockers and insults!
That I could forget the trickling tears and the blows of the
  bludgeons and hammers!
That I could look with a separate look on my own crucifixion
  and bloody crowning!

I remember. . . . I resume the overstaid fraction,
The grave of rock multiplies what has been confided to it. . . .
  or to any graves,
The corpses rise. . . . the gashes heal. . . . the fastenings roll
  away.

I troop forth replenished with supreme power, one of an
  average unending procession,
We walk the roads of Ohio and Massachusetts and Virginia
  and Wisconsin and New York and New Orleans and
  Texas and Montreal and San Francisco and Charleston
  and Savannah and Mexico,
Inland and by the seacoast and boundary lines. . . . and we
  pass the boundary lines.

Our swift ordinances are on their way over the whole earth,
The blossoms we wear in our hats are the growth of two
  thousand years.

Eleves I salute you,
I see the approach of your numberless gangs. . . . I see you
    understand yourselves and me,
And know that they who have eyes are divine, and the blind
    and lame are equally divine,
And that my steps drag behind yours yet go before them,
And are aware how I am with you no more than I am with
    everybody.

[39]
The friendly and flowing savage. . . . Who is he?
Is he waiting for civilization or past it and mastering it?

Is he some southwesterner raised outdoors? Is he Canadian?
Is he from the Mississippi country? or from Iowa, Oregon or
    California? or from the mountain? or prairie life of bush-
    life? or from the sea?

Wherever he goes men and women accept and desire him,
They desire he should like them and touch them and speak to
    them and stay with them.

Behaviour lawless as snow-flakes. . . . words simple as grass. . . .
    uncombed head and laughter and naivete;
Slowstepping feet and the common features, and the common
    modes and emanations,
They descend in new forms from the tips of his fingers,
They are wafted with the odor of his body or breath. . . . they
    fly out of the glance of his eyes.

Flaunt of the sunshine I need not your bask. . . . lie over,
You light surfaces only. . . . I force the surfaces and the depths
    also.

Earth! you seem to look for something at my hands,
Say old topknot! what do you want?

Man or woman! I might tell how I like you, but cannot,
And might tell what it is in me and what it is in you, but
    cannot,
And might tell the pinings I have. . . . the pulse of my nights
    and days.

Behold I do not give lectures or a little charity,
What I give I give out of myself.

You there, impotent, loose in the knees, open your scarfed
    chops till I blow grit within you,
Spread your palms and lift the flaps of your pockets,
I am not to be denied. . . . I compel. . . . I have stores plenty
    and to spare,
And any thing I have I bestow.

I do not ask who you are. . . . that is not important to me,
You can do nothing and be nothing but what I will infold you.

To a drudge of the cottonfields or emptier of privies I lean. . . .
    on his right cheek I put the family kiss,
And in my soul I swear I never will deny him.

On women fit for conception I start bigger and nimbler babes,
This day I am jetting the stuff of far more arrogant republics.

To any one dying. . . . thither I speed and twist the knob of the
        door,
Turn the bedclothes toward the foot of the bed,
Let the physician and the priest go home.

I seize the descending man. . . . I raise him with resistless will.

O despairer, here is my neck,
By God! you shall not go down! Hang your whole weight
        upon me.

I dilate you with tremendous breath. . . . I buoy you up;
Every room of the house do I fill with an armed force. . . .
        lovers of me, bafflers of graves:
Sleep! I and they keep guard all night;
Not doubt, not decease shall dare to lay finger upon you,
I have embraced you, and henceforth possess you to myself,
And when you rise in the morning you will find what I tell you
        is so.

[41]
I am he bringing help for the sick as they pant on their backs,
And for strong upright men I bring yet more needed help.

I heard what was said of the universe,
Heard it and heard of several thousand years;
It is middling well as far as it goes. . . . but is that all?

65

Magnifying and applying come I,

Outbidding at the start the old cautious hucksters,

The most they offer for mankind and eternity less than a spirt
of my own seminal wet,

Taking myself the exact dimensions of Jehovah and laying
them away,

Lithographing Kronos and Zeus his son, and Hercules his
grandson,

Buying drafts of Osiris and Isis and Belus and Brahma and
Adonai,

In my portfolio placing Manito loose, and Allah on a leaf,
and the crucifix engraved,

With Odin, and the hideous-faced Mexitli, and all idols and
images,

Honestly taking them all for what they are worth, and not a
cent more,

Admitting they were alive and did the work of their day,

Admitting they bore mites as for unfledged birds who have
now to rise and fly and sing for themselves,

Accepting the rough deific sketches to fill out better in
myself.... bestowing them freely on each man and
woman I see,

Discovering as much or more in a framer framing a house,

Putting higher claims for him there with his rolled-up sleeves,
driving the mallet and chisel;

Not objecting to special revelations.... considering a curl of
smoke or a hair on the back of my hand as curious as any
revelation;

Those ahold of fire-engines and hook-and-ladder ropes more
to me than the gods of the antique wars,
Minding their voices peal through the crash of destruction,
Their brawny limbs passing safe over charred laths. . . . their
white foreheads whole and unhurt out of the flames;
By the mechanic's wife with her babe at her nipple interceding
for every person born;
Three scythes at harvest whizzing in a row from three lusty
angels with shirts bagged out at their waists;
The snag-toothed hostler with red hair redeeming sins past and
to come,
Selling all he possesses and traveling on foot to fee lawyers for
his brother and sit by him while he is tried for forgery:
What was strewn in the amplest strewing the square rod about
me, and not filling the square rod then;
The bull and the bug never worshipped half enough,
Dung and dirt more admirable than was dreamed,
The supernatural of no account. . . . myself waiting my time to
be one of the supremes,
The day getting ready for me when I shall do as much good as
the best, and be as prodigious,
Guessing when I am it will not tickle me much to receive puffs
out of pulpit or print;
By my life-lumps! becoming already a creator!
Putting myself here and now to the ambushed womb of the
shadows!

. . . . A call in the midst of the crowd,
My own voice, orotund sweeping and final.

Come my children,
Come my boys and girls, and my women and household and
    intimates,
Now the performer launches his nerve. . . . he has passed his
    prelude on the reeds within.

Easily written loosefingered chords! I feel the thrum of their
    climax and close.

My head evolves on my neck,
Music rolls, but not from the organ. . . . folks are around me,
    but they are no household of mine.

Ever the hard and unsunk ground,
Ever the eaters and drinkers. . . . ever the upward and
    downward sun. . . . ever the air and the ceaseless tides,
Ever myself and my neighbors, refreshing and wicked and real,
Ever the old inexplicable query. . . . ever that thorned thumb—
    that breath of itches and thirsts,
Ever the vexer's hoot! hoot! till we find where the sly one hides
    and bring him forth;
Ever love. . . . ever the sobbing liquid of life,
Ever the bandage under the chin. . . . ever the trestles of death.

Here and there with dimes on the eyes walking,
To feed the greed of the belly the brains liberally spooning,

Tickets buying or taking or selling, but in to the feast never
once going;
Many sweating and ploughing and thrashing, and then the
chaff for payment receiving,
A few idly owning, and they the wheat continually claiming.

This is the city.... and I am one of the citizens;
Whatever interests the rest interests me.... politics, churches,
newspapers, schools,
Benevolent societies, improvements, banks, tariffs, steamships,
factories, markets,
Stocks and stores and real estate and personal estate.

They who piddle and patter here in collars and tailed
coats.... I am aware who they are.... and that they are
not worms or fleas,
I acknowledge the duplicates of myself under all the scrape-
lipped and pipe-legged concealments.

The weakest and shallowest is deathless with me,
What I do and say the same waits for them,
Every thought that flounders in me the same flounders in
them.

I know perfectly well my own egotism,
And know my omnivorous words, and cannot say any less,
And would fetch you whoever you are flush with myself.

My words are words of a questioning, and to indicate reality;

This printed and bound book. . . . but the printer and the printing-office boy?

The marriage estate and settlement. . . . but the body and mind of the bridegroom? also those of the bride?

The panorama of the sea. . . . but the sea itself?

The well-taken photographs. . . . but your wife or friend close and solid in your arms?

The fleet of ships of the line and all the modern improvements. . . . but the craft and pluck of the admiral?

The dishes and fare and furniture. . . . but the host and hostess, and the look out of their eyes?

The sky up there. . . . yet here or next door or across the way?

The saints and sages in history. . . . but you yourself?

Sermons and creeds and theology. . . . but the human brain, and what is called reason, and what is called love, and what is called life?

[43]

I do not despise you priests;

My faith is the greatest of faiths and the least of faiths,

Enclosing all worship ancient and modern, and all between ancient and modern,

Believing I shall come again upon the earth after five thousand years,

Waiting responses from oracles. . . . honoring the gods. . . . saluting the sun,

Making a fetish of the first rock or stump. . . . powowing with sticks in the circle of obis,

Helping the lama or brahmin as he trims the lamps of the
   idols,
Dancing yet through the streets in a phallic procession. . . .
   rapt and austere in the woods, a gymnosophist,
Drinking mead from the skull-cup. . . . to shasta and vedas
   admirant. . . . minding the koran,
Walking the teokallis, spotted with gore from the stone and
   knife—beating the serpent-skin drum;
Accepting the gospels, accepting him that was crucified,
   knowing assuredly that he is divine,
To the mass kneeling—to the puritan's prayer rising—sitting
   patiently in a pew,
Ranting and frothing in my insane crisis—waiting dead-like till
   my spirit arouses me;
Looking forth on pavement and land, and outside of pavement
   and land,
Belonging to the winders of the circuit of circuits.

One of that centripetal and centrifugal gang,
I turn and talk like a man leaving charges before a journey.

Down-hearted doubters, dull and excluded,
Frivolous sullen moping angry affected disheartened
   atheistical,
I know every one of you, and know the unspoken
   interrogatories,
By experience I know them.

How the flukes splash!

How they contort rapid as lightning, with spasms and spouts
of blood!

Be at peace bloody flukes of doubters and sullen mopers,
I take my place among you as much as among any;
The past is the push of you and me and all precisely the same,
And the day and night are for you and me and all,
And what is yet untried and afterward is for you and me and
all.

I do not know what is untried and afterward,
But I know it is sure and alive and sufficient.

Each who passes is considered, and each who stops is
considered, and not a single one can it fail.

It cannot fail the young man who died and was buried,
Nor the young woman who died and was put by his side,
Not the little child that peeped in at the door and then drew
back and was never seen again,
Nor the old man who has lived without purpose, and feels it
with bitterness worse than gall,
Nor him in the poorhouse tubercled by rum and the bad
disorder,
Nor the numberless slaughtered and wrecked.... nor the
brutish koboo, called the ordure of humanity,
Nor the sacs merely floating with open mouths for food to slip
in,
Nor any thing in the earth, or down in the oldest graves of the
earth,

Nor any thing in the myriads of spheres, nor one of the
    myriads of myriads that inhabit them,
Nor the present, nor the least wisp that is known.

[44]
It is time to explain myself.... let us stand up.

What is known I strip away.... I launch all men and women
    forward with me into the unknown.

The clock indicates the moment.... but what does eternity
    indicate?

Eternity lies in bottomless reservoirs.... its buckets are rising
    forever and ever,
They pour and they pour and they exhale away.

We have thus far exhausted trillions of winters and summers;
There are trillions ahead, and trillions ahead of them.

Births have brought us richness and variety,
And other births will bring us richness and variety.

I do not call one greater and one smaller,
That which fills its period and place is equal to any.

Were mankind murderous or jealous upon you my brother or
    my sister?
I am sorry for you.... they are not murderous or jealous
    upon me;

All has been gentle with me. . . . I keep no account with
  lamentation;
What have I to do with lamentation?

I am an acme of things accomplished, and I an encloser of
  things to be.

My feet strike an apex of the apices of the stairs,
On every step bunches of ages, and larger bunches between the
  steps,
All below duly traveled—and still I mount and mount.

Rise after rise bow the phantoms behind me,
Afar down I see the huge first Nothing, the vapor from the
  nostrils of death,
I know I was even there. . . . I waited unseen and always,
And slept while God carried me through the lethargic mist,
And took my time. . . . and took no hurt from the foetid
  carbon.

Long I was hugged close. . . . long and long.

Immense have been the preparations for me,
Faithful and friendly the arms that have helped me.

Cycles ferried my cradle, rowing and rowing like cheerful
  boatmen;
For room to me stars kept aside in their own rings,
They sent influences to look after what was to hold me.

Before I was born out of my mother generations guided me,

My embryo has never been torpid. . . . nothing could overlay
    it;
For it the nebula cohered to an orb. . . . the long slow strata
    piled to rest it on. . . . vast vegetables gave it sustenance,
Monstrous sauroids transported it in their mouths and
    deposited it with care.

All forces have been steadily employed to complete and delight
    me,
Now I stand on this spot with my soul.

[45]
Span of youth! Ever-pushed elasticity! Manhood balanced and
    florid and full!

My lovers suffocate me!
Crowding my lips, and thick in the pores of my skin,
Jostling me through streets and public halls. . . . coming naked
    to me at night,
Crying by day Ahoy from the rocks of the river. . . . swinging
    and chirping over my head,
Calling my name from flowerbeds or vines or tangled
    underbrush,
Or while I swim in the bath. . . . or drink from the pump at
    the corner. . . . or the curtain is down at the opera. . . . or
    I glimpse at a woman's face in the railroad car;
Lighting on every moment of my life,
Bussing my body with soft and balsamic busses,

75

Noiselessly passing handfuls out of their hearts and giving
them to be mine.

Old age superbly rising! Ineffable grace of dying days!

Every condition promulges not only itself. . . . it promulges
what grows after and out of itself,
And the dark hush promulges as much as any.

I open my scuttle at night and see the far-sprinkled systems,
And all I see, multiplied as high as I can cipher, edge but the
rim of the farther systems.

Wider and wider they spread, expanding and always expand-
ing,
Outward and outward and forever outward.

My sun has his sun, and round him obediently wheels,
He joins with his partners a group of superior circuit,
And greater sets follow, making specks of the greatest inside
them.

There is no stoppage, and never can be stoppage;
If I and you and the worlds and all beneath or upon their
surfaces, and all the palpable life, were this moment
reduced back to a pallid float, it would not avail in the
long run,
We should surely bring up again where we now stand,
And as surely go as much farther, and then farther and farther.

A few quadrillions of eras, a few octillions of cubic leagues, do
    not hazard the span, or make it impatient,
They are but parts. . . . any thing is but a part.

See ever so far. . . . there is limitless space outside of that,
Count ever so much. . . . there is limitless time around that.

Our rendezvous is fitly appointed. . . . God will be there and
    wait till we come.

[46]
I know I have the best of time and space—and that I was never
    measured, and never will be measured.

I tramp a perpetual journey,
My signs are a rain-proof coat and good shoes and a staff cut
    from the woods;
No friend of mine takes his ease in my chair,
I have no chair, nor church nor philosophy;
I lead no man to a dinner-table or library or exchange,
But each man and each woman of you I lead upon a knoll,
My left hand hooks you round the waist,
My right hand points to landscapes of continents, and a plain
    public road.

Not I, not any one else can travel that road for you,
You must travel it for yourself.

It is not far. . . . it is within reach,

Perhaps you have been on it since you were born, and did not
    know,
Perhaps it is every where on water and on land.

Shoulder your duds, and I will mine, and let us hasten forth;
Wonderful cities and free nations we shall fetch as we go.

If you tire, give me both burdens, and rest the chuff of your
    hand on my hip,
And in due time you shall repay the same service to me;
For after we start we never lie by again.

This day before dawn I ascended a hill and looked at the
    crowded heaven,
And I said to my spirit, When we become the enfolders of
    those orbs and the pleasure and knowledge of every thing
    in them, shall we be filled and satisfied then?
And my spirit said No, we level that lift to pass and continue
    beyond.

You are also asking me questions, and I hear you;
I answer that I cannot answer. . . . you must find out for
    yourself.

Sit awhile wayfarer,
Here are biscuits to eat and here is milk to drink,
But as soon as you sleep and renew yourself in sweet clothes
    I will certainly kiss you with my goodbye kiss and open
    the gate for your egress hence.

Long enough have you dreamed contemptible dreams,

Now I wash the gum from your eyes,
You must habit yourself to the dazzle of the light and of every
    moment of your life.

Long have you timidly waded, holding a plank by the shore,
Now I will you to be a bold swimmer,
To jump off in the midst of the sea, and rise again and nod to
    me and shout, and laughingly dash with your hair.

[47]
I am the teacher of athletes,
He that by me spreads a wider breast than my own proves the
    width of my own,
He most honors my style who learns under it to destroy the
    teacher.

The boy I love, the same becomes a man not through derived
    power but in his own right,
Wicked, rather than virtuous out of conformity or fear,
Fond of his sweetheart, relishing well his steak,
Unrequited love or a slight cutting him worse than a wound
    cuts,
First rate to ride, to fight, to hit the bull's eye, to sail a skiff,
    to sing a song or play on the banjo,
Preferring scars and faces pitted with smallpox over all
    latherers and those that keep out of the sun.

I teach straying from me, yet who can stray from me?
I follow you whoever you are from the present hour;

My words itch at your ears till you understand them.

I do not say these things for a dollar, or to fill up the time
     while I wait for a boat;
It is you talking just as much as myself. . . . I act as the tongue
     of you,
It was tied in your mouth. . . . in mine it begins to be loosened.

I swear I will never mention love or death inside a house,
And I swear I never will translate myself at all, only to him or
     her who privately stays with me in the open air.

If you would understand me go to the heights or water-shore,
The nearest gnat is an explanation and a drop or the motion
     of waves a key,
The maul the oar and the handsaw second my words.

No shuttered room or school can commune with me,
But roughs and little children better than they.

The young mechanic is closest to me. . . . he knows me pretty
     well,
The woodman that takes his axe and jug with him shall take
     me with him all day,
The farmboy ploughing in the field feels good at the sound of
     my voice,
In vessels that sail my words must sail. . . . I go with fishermen
     and seamen, and love them,
My face rubs to the hunter's face when he lies down alone in
     his blanket,

The driver thinking of me does not mind the jolt of his wagon,
The young mother and old mother shall comprehend me,
The girl and the wife rest the needle a moment and forget
    where they are,
They and all would resume what I have told them.

[48]
I have said that the soul is not more than the body,
And I have said that the body is not more than the soul,
And nothing, not God, is greater to one than one's-self is,
And whoever walks a furlong without sympathy walks to his
    own funeral, dressed in his shroud,
And I or you pocketless of a dime may purchase the pick of
    the earth,
And to glance with an eye or show a bean in its pod
    confounds the learning of all times,
And there is no trade or employment but the young man
    following it may become a hero,
And there is no object so soft but it makes a hub for the
    wheeled universe,
And any man or woman shall stand cool and supercilious
    before a million universes.

And I call to mankind, Be not curious about God,
For I who am curious about each am not curious about
    God,
No array of terms can say how much I am at peace about
    God and about death.

I hear and behold God in every object, yet I understand God
    not in the least,
Nor do I understand who there can be more wonderful than
    myself.

Why should I wish to see God better than this day?
I see something of God each hour of the twenty-four, and each
    moment then,
In the faces of men and women I see God, and in my own face
    in the glass;
I find letters from God dropped in the street, and every one is
    signed by God's name,
And I leave them where they are, for I know that others will
    punctually come forever and ever.

[49]
And as to you death, and you bitter hug of mortality. . . . it is
    idle to try to alarm me.

To his work without flinching the accoucheur comes,
I see the elderhand pressing receiving supporting,
I recline by the sills of the exquisite flexible doors. . . . and
    mark the outlet, and mark the relief and escape.

And as to you corpse I think you are good manure, but that
    does not offend me,
I smell the white roses sweetscented and growing,
I reach to the leafy lips. . . . I reach to the polished breasts of
    melons,

And as to you life, I reckon you are the leavings of many
    deaths,
No doubt I have died myself ten thousand times before.

I hear you whispering there O stars of heaven,
O suns. . . . O grass of graves. . . . O perpetual transfers and
    promotions. . . . if you do not say anything how can I say
    anything?

Of the turbid pool that lies in the autumn forest,
Of the moon that descends the steeps of the soughing twilight,
Toss, sparkles of day and dusk. . . . toss on the black stems
    that decay in the muck,
Toss to the moaning gibberish of the dry limbs.

I ascend from the moon. . . . I ascend from the night,
And perceive of the ghastly glitter the sunbeams reflected,
And debouch to the steady and central from the offspring
    great or small.

[50]
There is that in me. . . . I do not know what it is. . . . but I
    know it is in me.

Wrenched and sweaty. . . . calm and cool then my body
    becomes;
I sleep. . . . I sleep long.

I do not know it. . . . it is without name. . . . it is a word
    unsaid,

It is not in any dictionary or utterance or symbol.

Something it swings on more than the earth I swing on,
To it the creation is the friend whose embracing awakes me.

Perhaps I might tell more. . . . Outlines! I plead for my
    brothers and sisters.

Do you see O my brothers and sisters?
It is not chaos or death. . . . it is form and union and plan. . . .
    it is eternal life. . . . it is happiness.

[51]
The past and present wilt. . . . I have filled them and emptied
    them,
And proceed to fill my next fold of the future.

Listener up there! Here you. . . . what have you to confide to me?
Look in my face while I snuff the sidle of evening,
Talk honestly, for no one else hears you, and I stay only a
    minute longer.

Do I contradict myself?
Very well then. . . . I contradict myself;
I am large. . . . I contain multitudes.

I concentrate toward them that are nigh. . . . I wait on the
    door-slab.

Who has done his day's work and will soonest be through with
    his supper?

Who wishes to walk with me?

Will you speak before I am gone? Will you prove already too
late?

[52]
The spotted hawk swoops by and accuses me. . . . he
complains of my gab and my loitering.

I too am not a bit tamed. . . . I too am untranslatable,
I sound my barbaric yawp over the roofs of the world.

The last scud of day holds back for me,
It flings my likeness after the rest and true as any on the
shadowed wilds,
It coaxes me to the vapor and the dusk.

I depart as air. . . . I shake my white locks at the runaway sun,
I effuse my flesh in eddies and drift it in lacy jags.

I bequeath myself to the dirt to grow from the grass I love,
If you want me again look for me under your bootsoles.

You will hardly know who I am or what I mean,
But I shall be good health to you nevertheless,
And filter and fibre your blood.

Failing to fetch me at first keep encouraged,
Missing me one place search another,
I stop some where waiting for you

PENGUIN 60s CLASSICS

READ MORE IN PENGUIN

For complete information about books available from Penguin and how to order them, please write to us at the appropriate address below. Please note that for copyright reasons the selection of books varies from country to country.

IN THE UNITED KINGDOM: Please write to *Dept. EP, Penguin Books Ltd, Bath Road, Harmondsworth, Middlesex UB7 0DA.*

IN THE UNITED STATES: Please write to *Consumer Sales, Penguin USA, P.O. Box 999, Dept. 17109, Bergenfield, New Jersey 07621-0120.* VISA and MasterCard holders call 1-800-253-6476 to order Penguin titles.

IN CANADA: Please write to *Penguin Books Canada Ltd, 10 Alcorn Avenue, Suite 300, Toronto, Ontario M4V 3B2.*

IN AUSTRALIA: Please write to *Penguin Books Australia Ltd, P.O. Box 257, Ringwood, Victoria 3134.*

IN NEW ZEALAND: Please write to *Penguin Books (NZ) Ltd, Private Bag 102902, North Shore Mail Centre, Auckland 10.*

IN INDIA: Please write to *Penguin Books India Pvt Ltd, 706 Eros Apartments, 56 Nehru Place, New Delhi 110 019.*

IN THE NETHERLANDS: Please write to *Penguin Books Netherlands bv, Postbus 3507, NL-1001 AH Amsterdam.*

IN GERMANY: Please write to *Penguin Books Deutschland GmbH, Metzlerstrasse 26, 60594 Frankfurt am Main.*

IN SPAIN: Please write to *Penguin Books S. A., Bravo Murillo 19, 1° B, 28015 Madrid.*

IN ITALY: Please write to *Penguin Italia s.r.l., Via Felice Casati 20, I–20124 Milano.*

IN FRANCE: Please write to *Penguin France S. A., 17 rue Lejeune, F–31000 Toulouse.*

IN JAPAN: Please write to *Penguin Books Japan, Ishikiribashi Building, 2–5–4, Suido, Bunkyo-ku, Tokyo 112.*

IN GREECE: Please write to *Penguin Hellas Ltd, Dimocritou 3, GR–106 71 Athens.*

IN SOUTH AFRICA: Please write to *Longman Penguin Southern Africa (Pty) Ltd, Private Bag X08, Bertsham 2013.*